Proverbs According to Ruggles

CINDY BUNCH and DOUG HALL

Tyndale House Publishers, Inc. • Wheaton, Illinois

Copyright © 1993 by Tyndale House Publishers, Inc.
All rights reserved

Library of Congress Cataloging-in-Publication Data

Bunch, Cindy.
   Proverbs according to Ruggles / Cindy Bunch and Doug Hall.
     p. cm.
   ISBN 0-8423-1049-5
   1. Hall, Doug, date.   2. Proverbs, American—Caricatures and cartoons.   3. Dogs—Caricatures and cartoons.   4. American wit and humor, Pictorial.   I. Hall, Doug, date.   II. Title.
NC1429.H323A4   1993
741.5′973—dc20
                                                                               93-16609

Printed in the United States of America

98   98   96   95   94   93
9   8   7   6   5   4   3   2   1

Don't hide your affection.

Let nothing stand in the way of your pursuit of truth.

Be patient.

Ask and it will be given to you.

Be persistent.

There's a time to plant

...and a time to uproot.

Welcome guests.

Share interests with that special person in your life.

ur sins will find you out.

Repent of your sins.

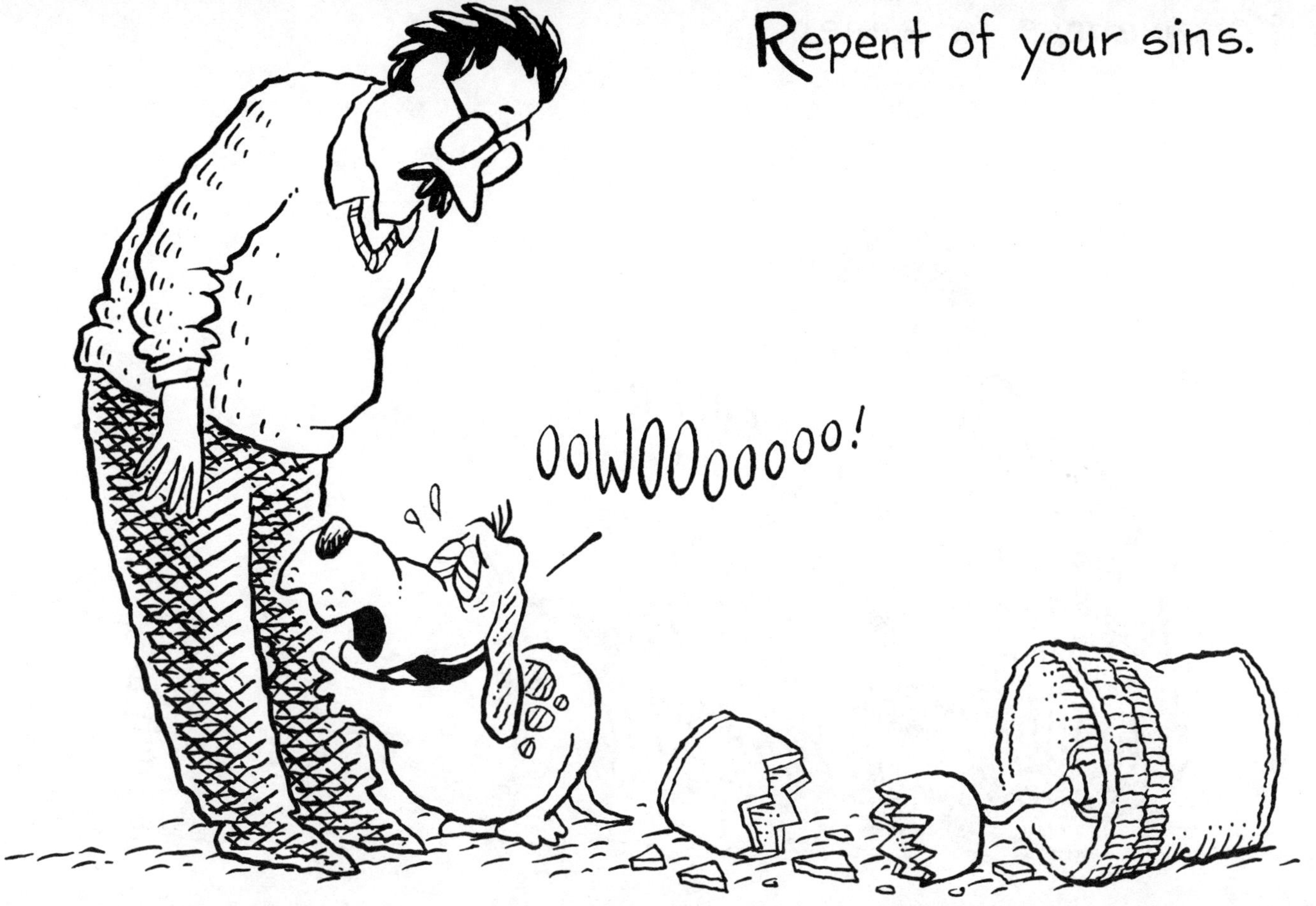

Forgiveness is sweet.

SCRATCH
SCRATCH

Show concern for others.

FLEA COLLAR

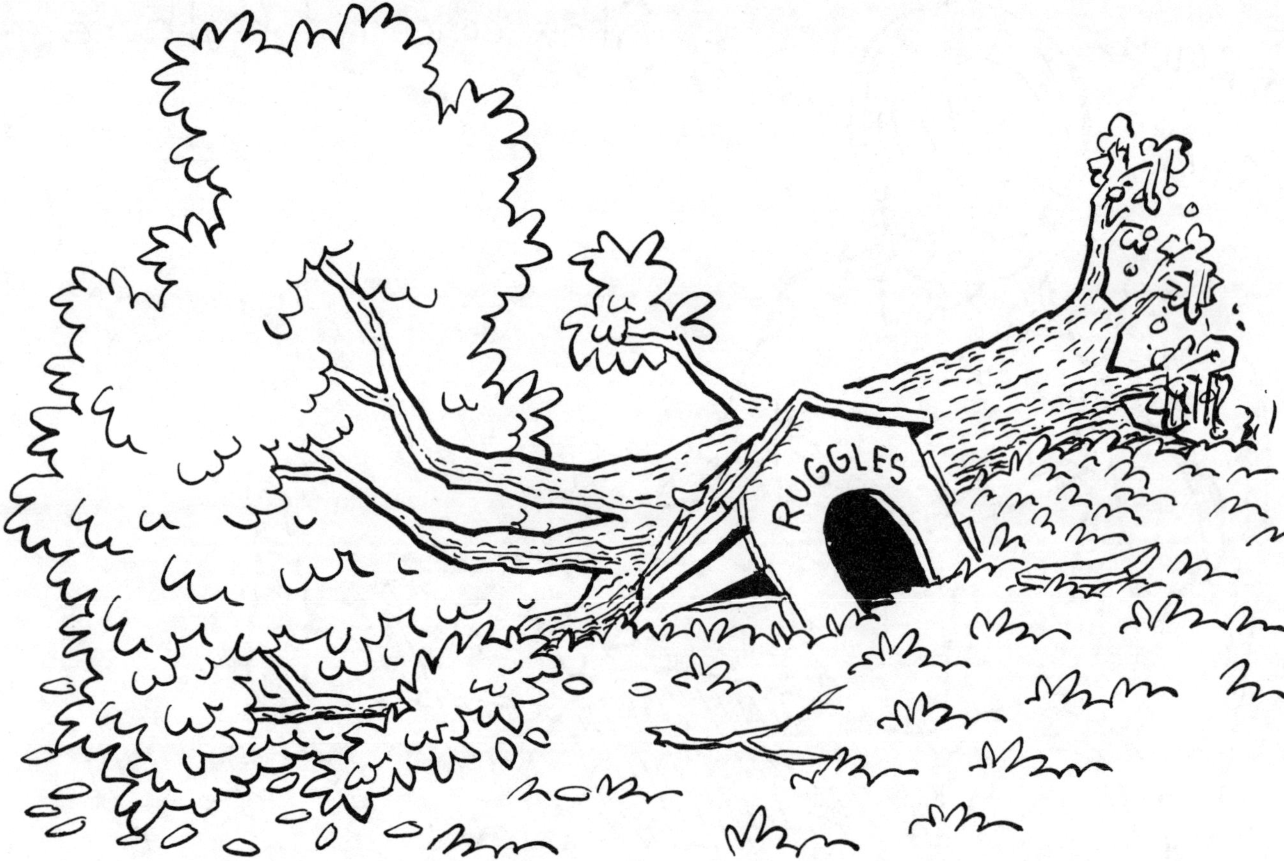
RUGGLES

Know where to find security.

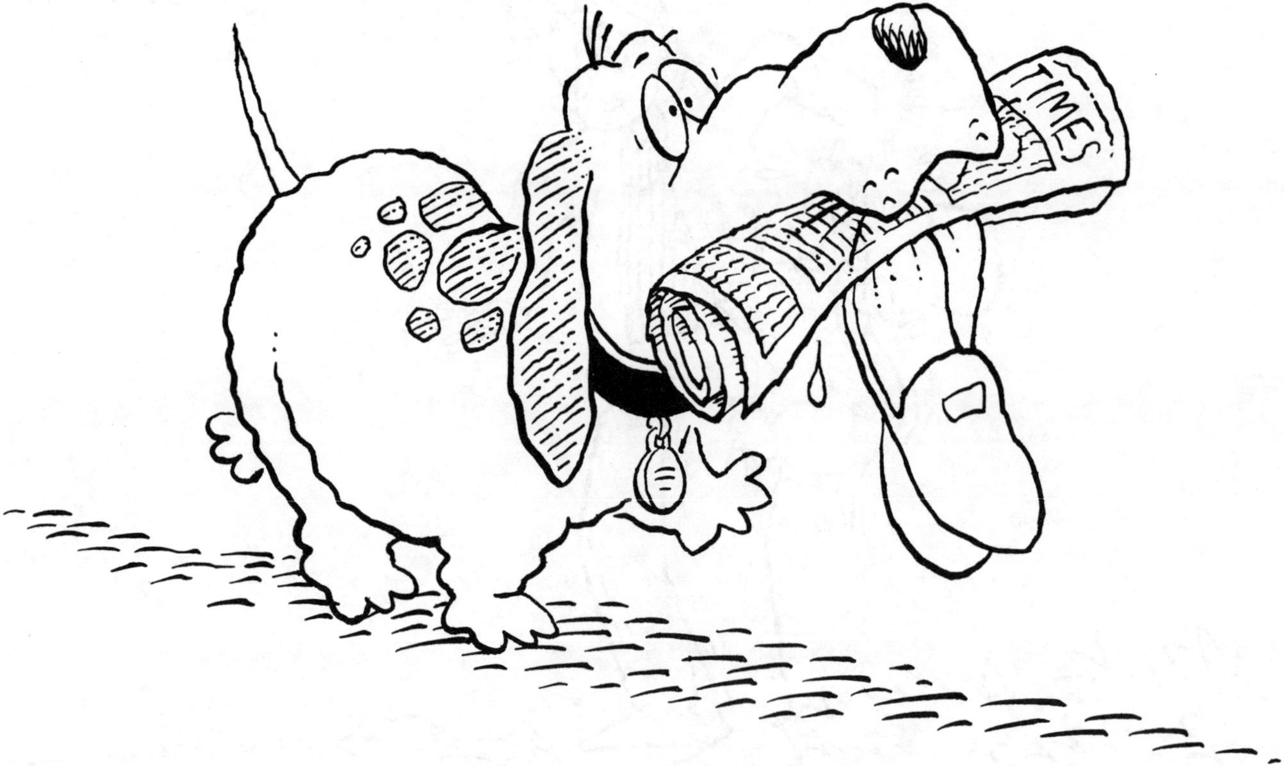
TIMES

Serve humbly and expect no reward.

See life as a child.

Appreciate cultural diversity.

Know when you're not welcome.

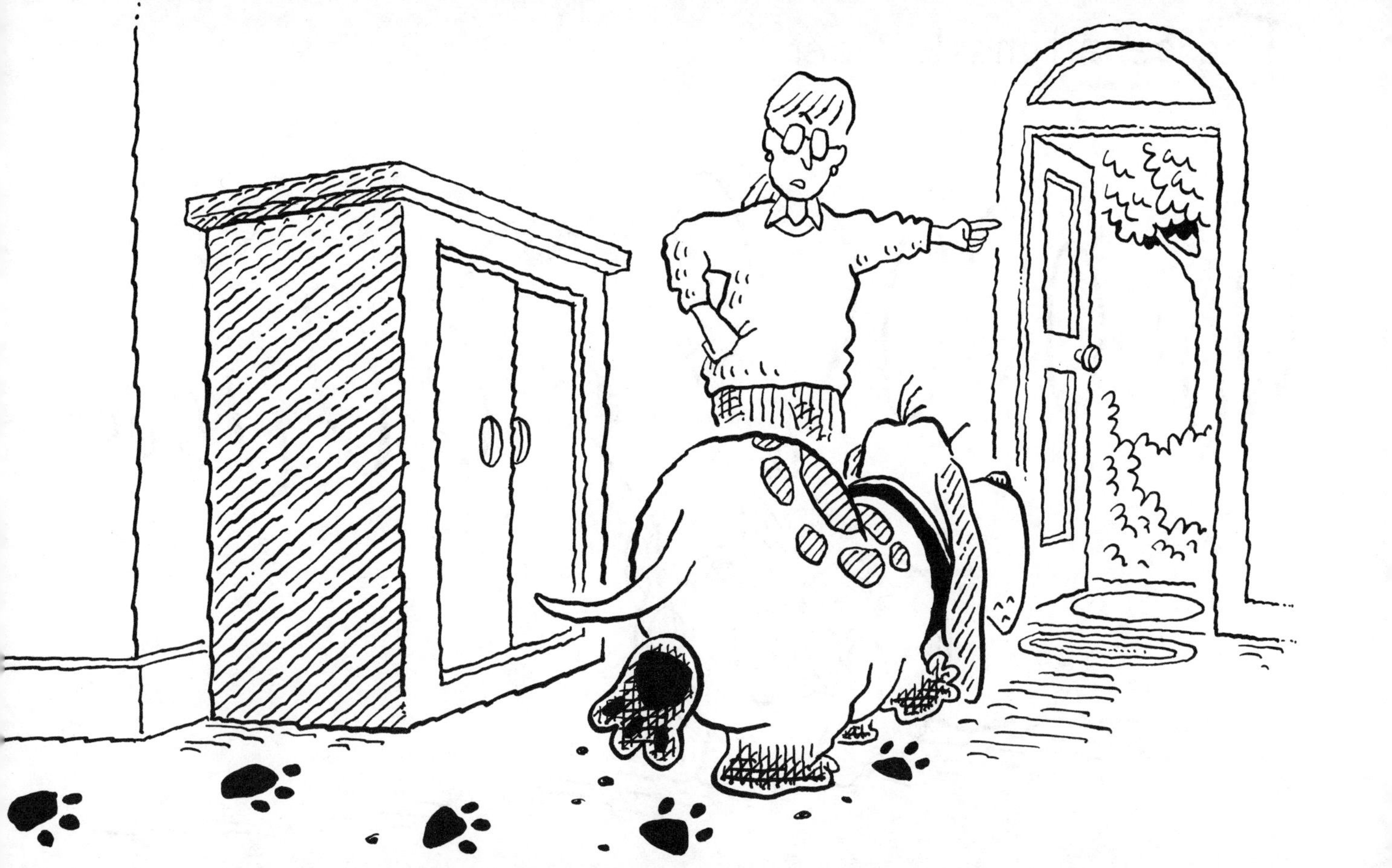

There's a time to weep

WOOOOOOOOOOOOOOOooo

...and a time to laugh.

Protect those you love.

Make time for friends.

Be forgiving.

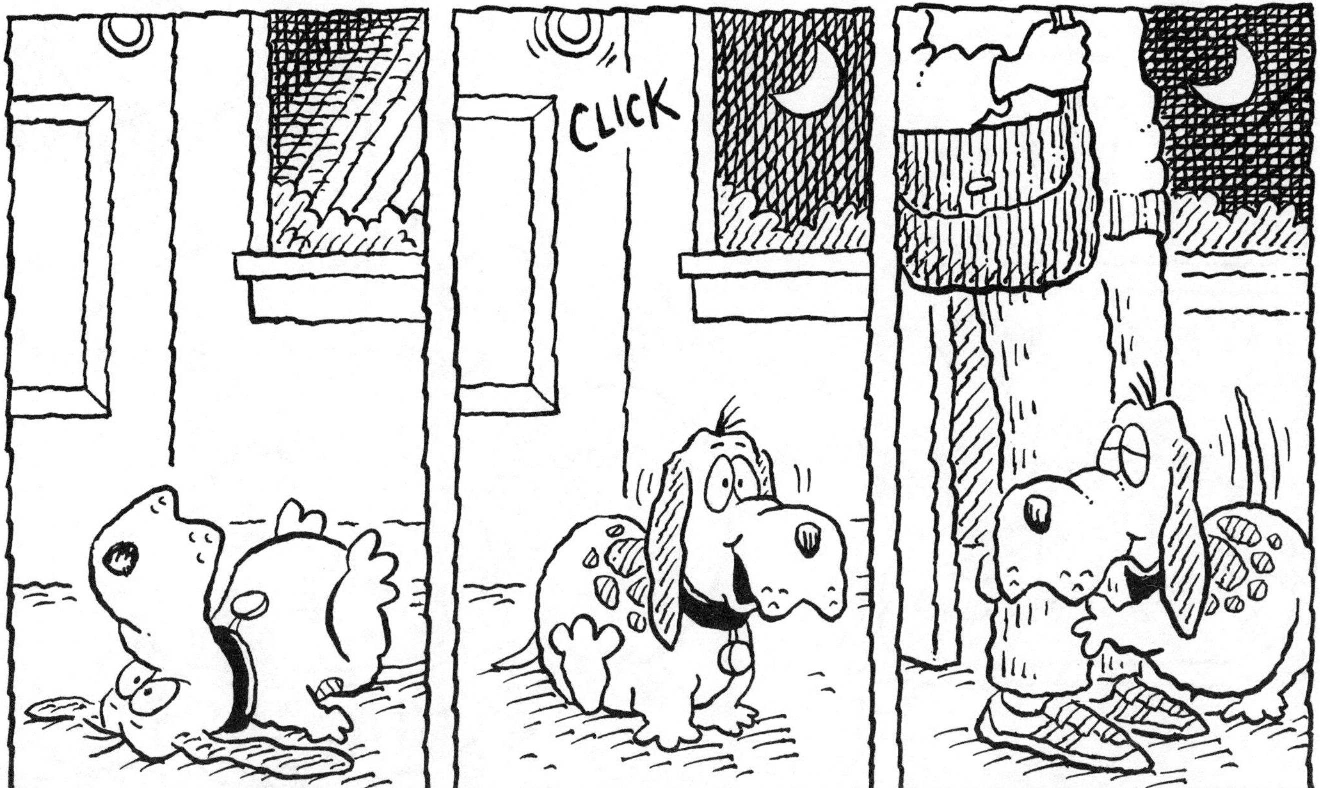
CLICK

There's a time for everything.

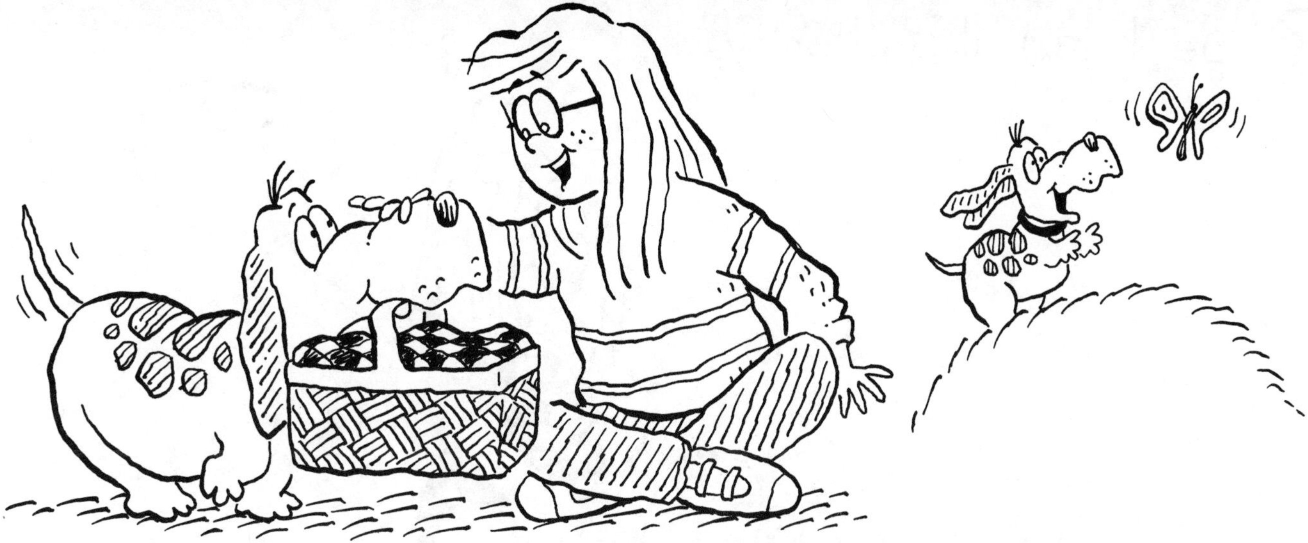

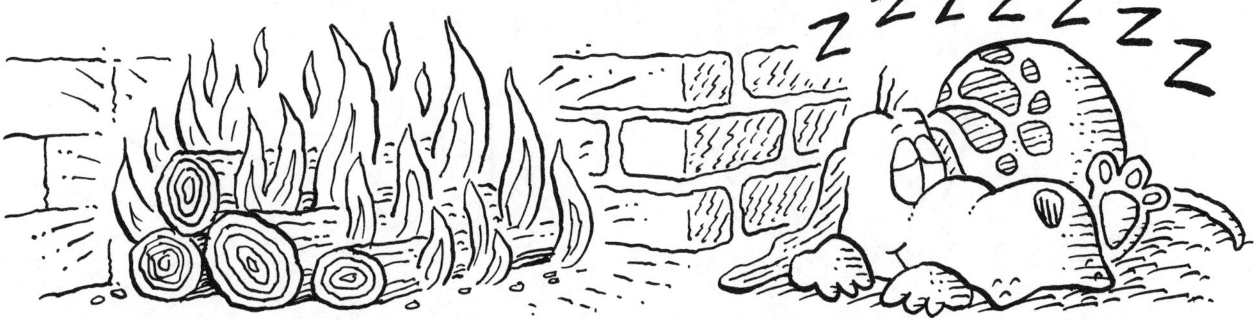
ZZZZZZZ

Respect lawful authority.

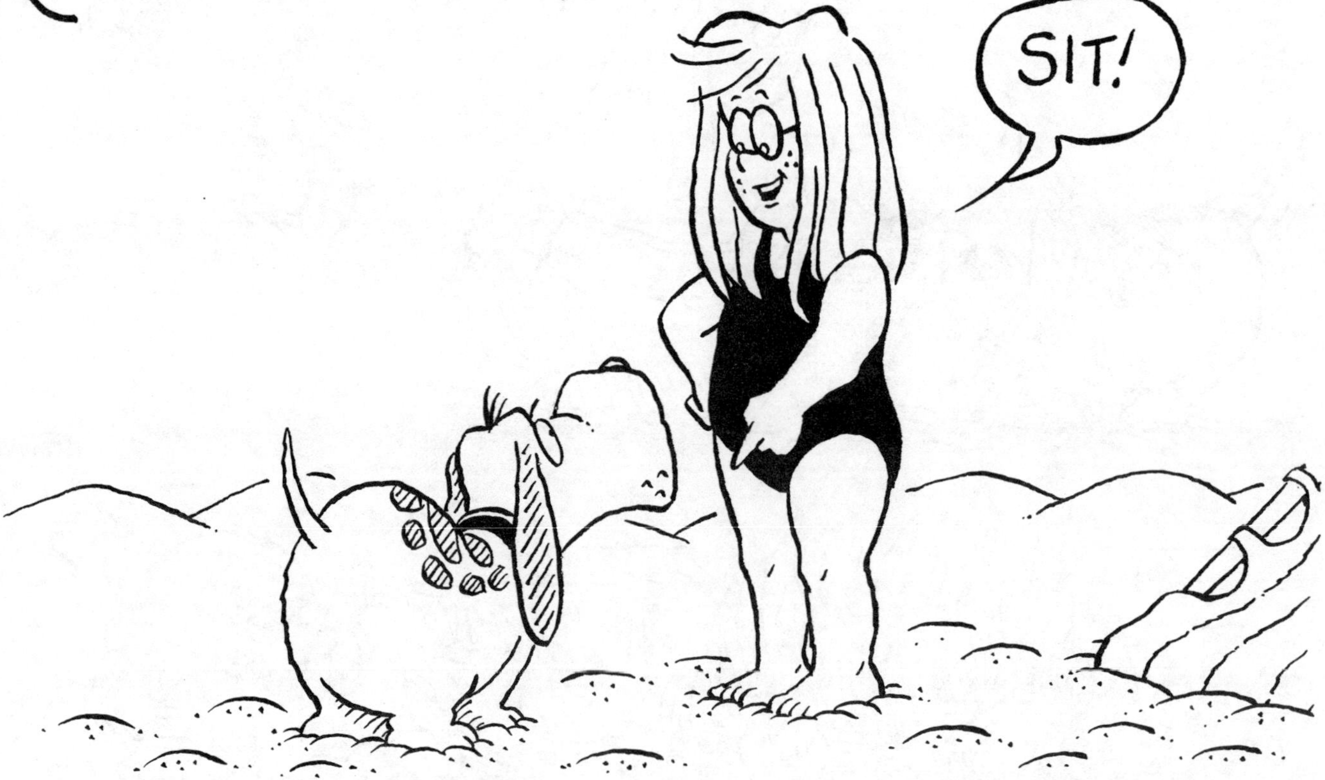

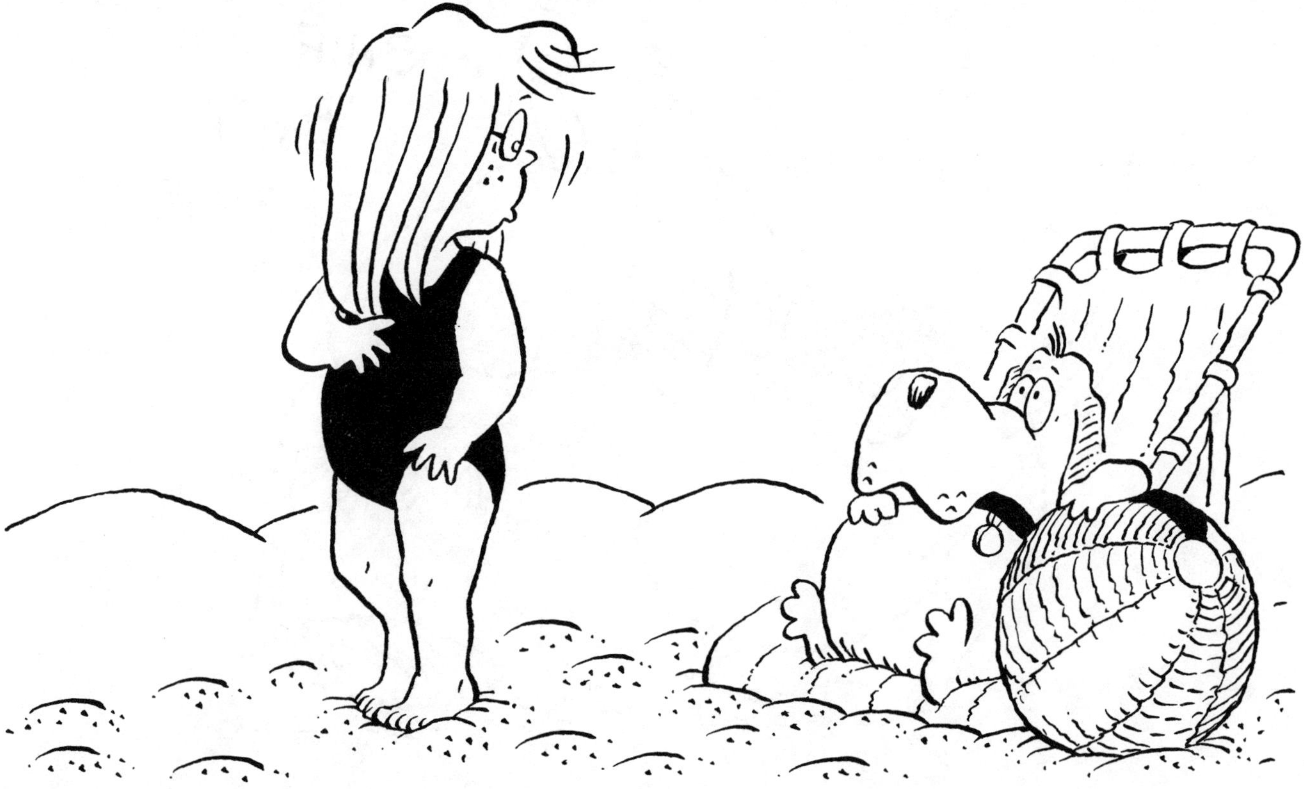

Be inquisitive

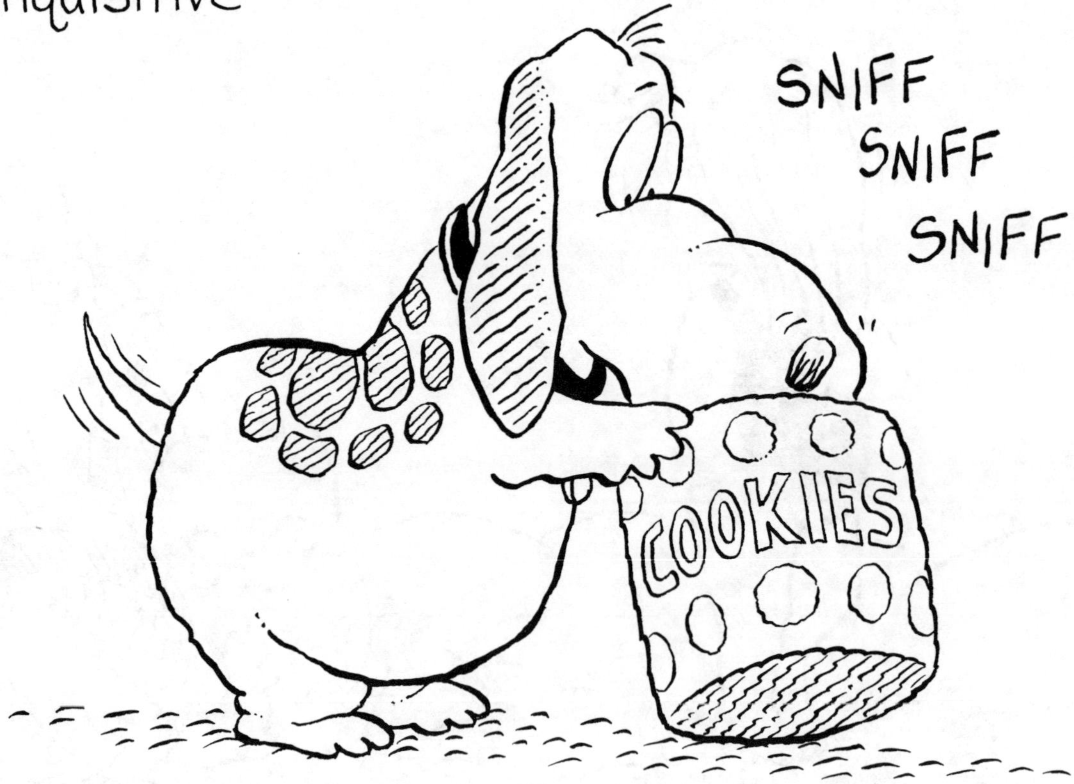

...but use good judgment.

Trust others.

Be thankful for what you are given.

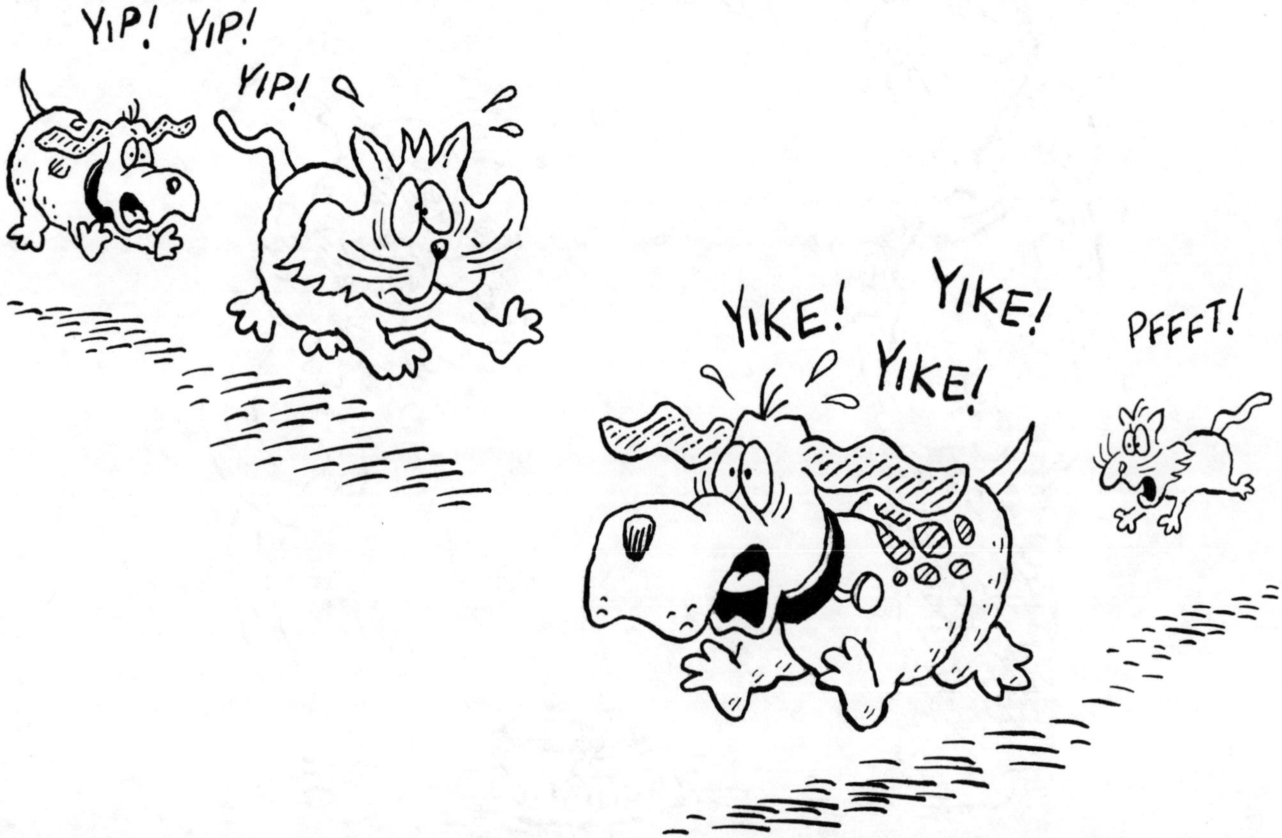
YIP! YIP!
YIP!
YIKE!
YIKE!
YIKE!
PFFFT!

Make peace with your enemies.

Give relationships priority.

Be modest.

There's a time to be silent.

... and a time to speak.

Develop your talents.

Be prepared for the end.

When friends are together, there's never a crowd.

Be at peace with all creatures.

Respect your elders.

Be gentle.

Show proper humility.

Know when to be proud.

Appreciate simple pleasures.

Be casual.

There's a time to keep

...and a time to throw away.

Never let your mind grow old.

Enjoy creation.

Express love to everyone.

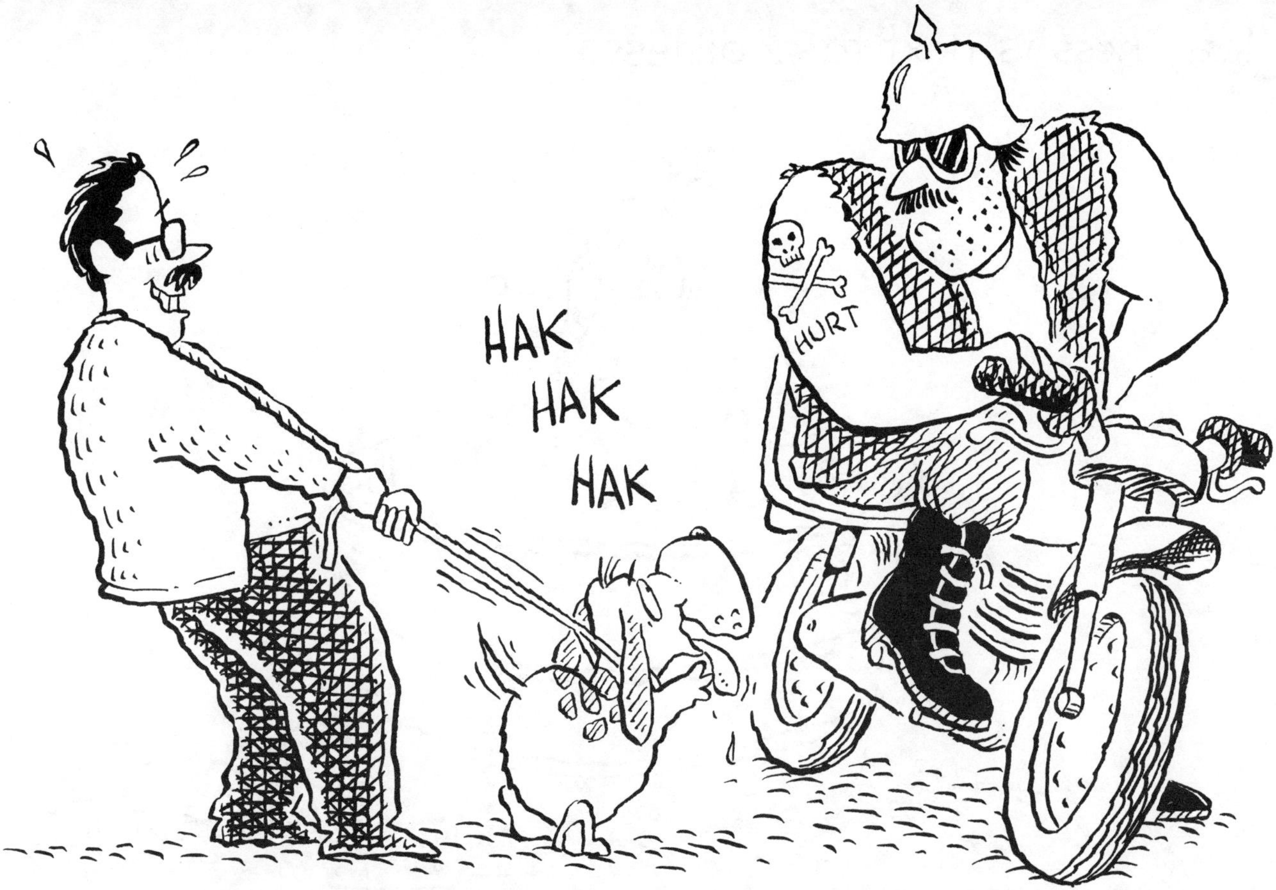
HAK
HAK
HAK
HURT

Cleanliness is next to godliness.

But then, Jesus never said that.

Celebrate sacred days.

Don't worry about what you wear.

Comfort those in need.

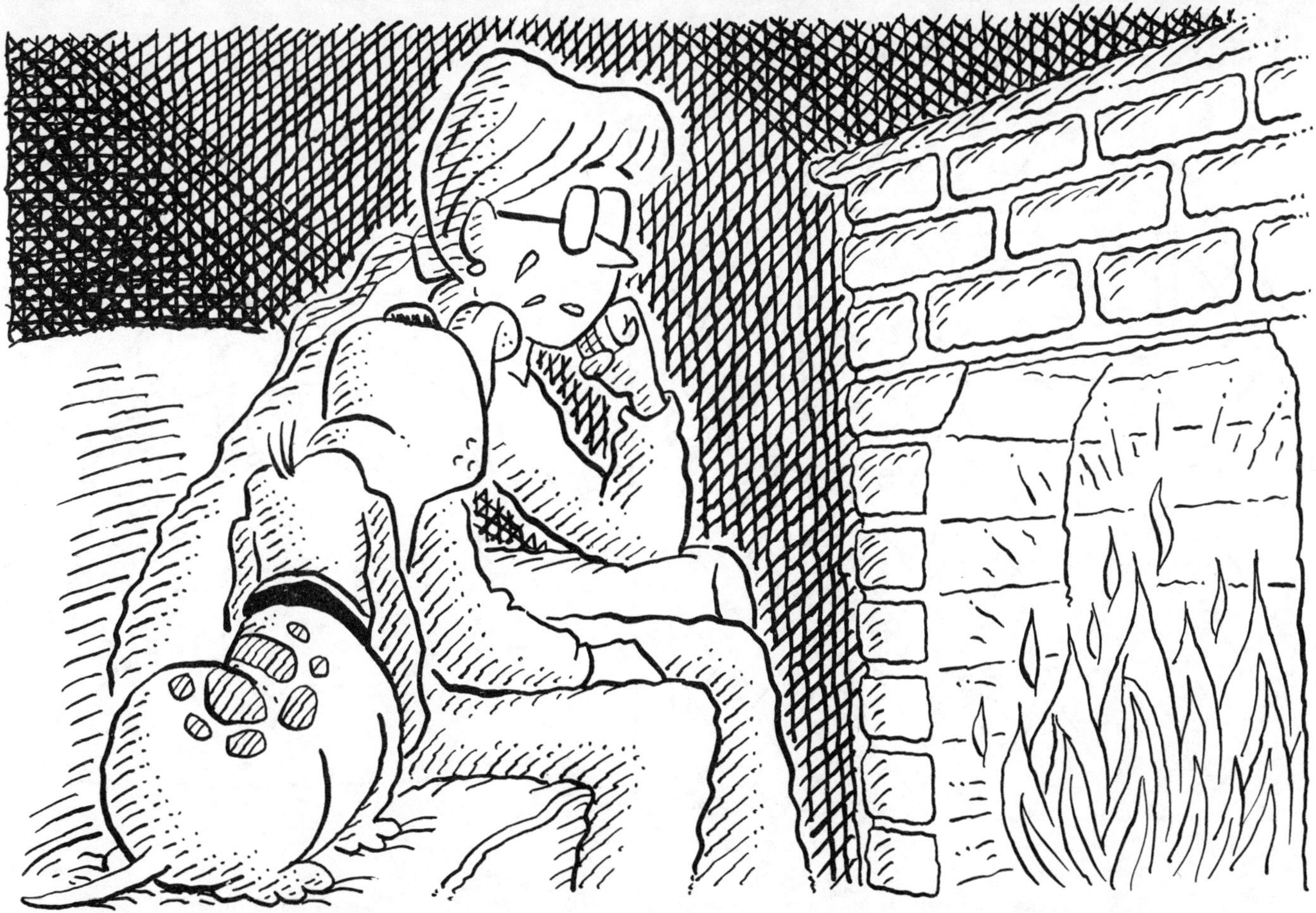

There's a time to mourn.

...and a time to dance.

Make yourself indispensable.

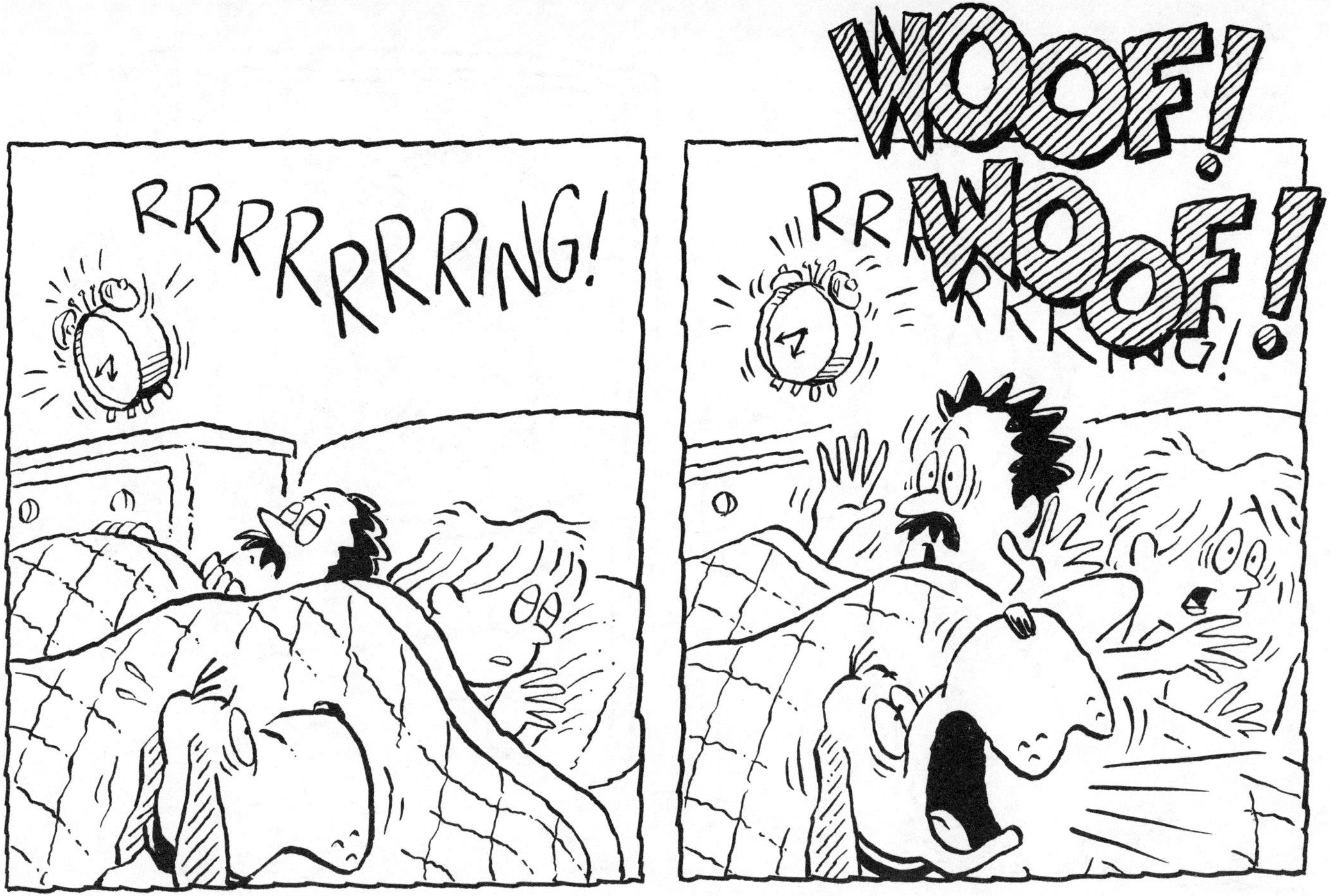
RRRRRRRING!
WOOF!
WOOF!

Confront evil.

WOOF! WOOF! WOOF!

Express your needs.

Be self-controlled.

Know your limits.

Always be ready to help.

Put others first.

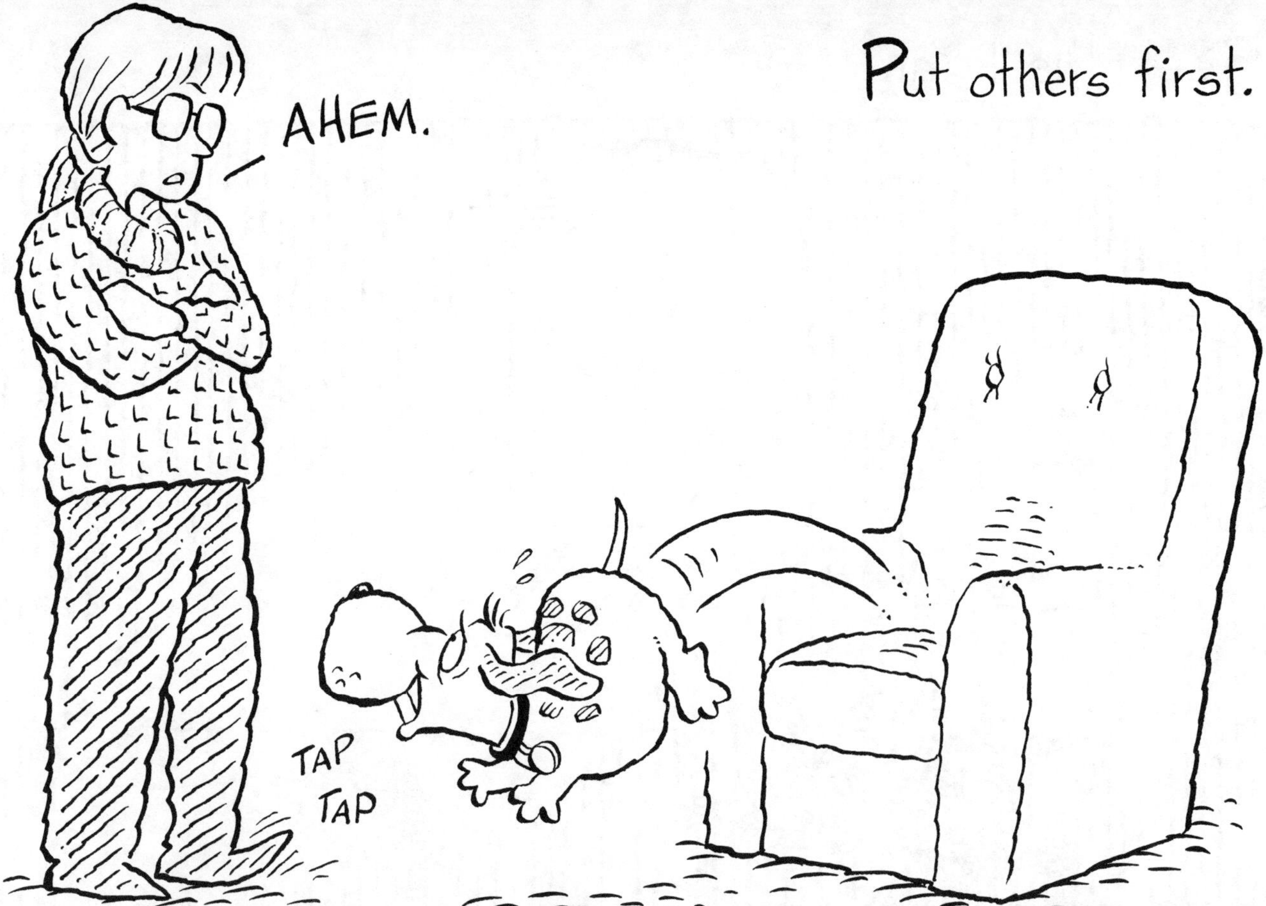

Seek the light.

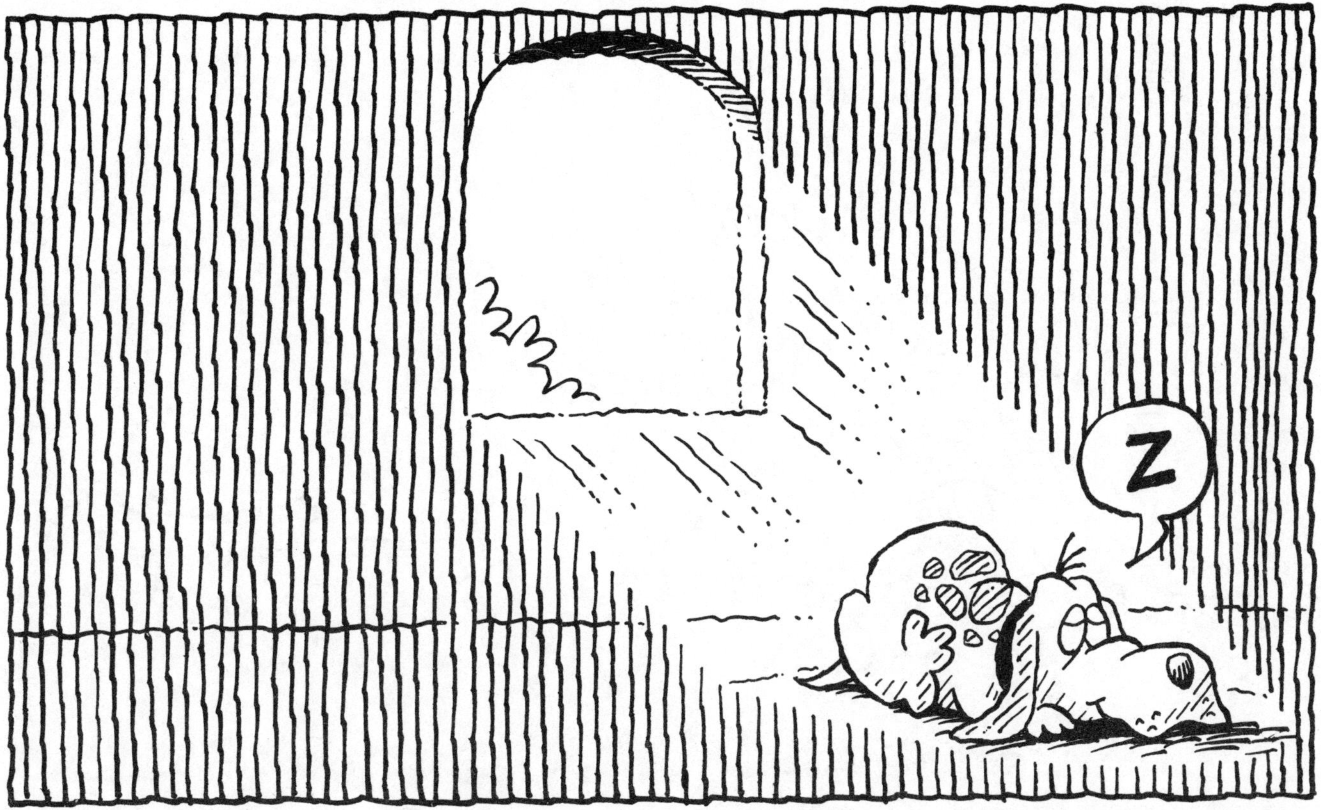
Z

Never give up hope

... or surrender your optimism.

Look for the good in everything.